T0062888

365 Days Of Mindfulness

365 Days Of Mindfulness

Quotes For Life

Pooja Shende

PARTRIDGE

Print information available on the last page.

To order additional copies of this book, contact
Partridge India
000 800 10062 62
orders.india@partridgepublishing.com

www.partridgepublishing.com/india

Acknowledgement

It takes me immense pleasure to dedicate this book to you, "The Reader" and all the lovely people who are with me on this wonderful journey of life.

This book is also dedicated to each and every person involved in getting this book published and making it available to millions and billions of people all over the world.

This book is also dedicated to all my lovely and ever supporting family and friends who have been with me on this wonderful journey of life.

This book is also dedicated to my parents, my sisters, my son, my husband and my lovely friend Jayshree who have always been so loving, caring, supporting and the strongest pillars of my life. I am blessed to have them in my life.

I love you all.

I take this opportunity to thank you God and The Universe for everything!

About the Author

Pooja Shende is the Founder of Lotus Soul 9.

After a successful corporate career with an experience of 20 plus years, she is an Entrepreneur, Author, Practitioner of Emotional Intelligence, Practitioner of NLP and a Performance Coach.

She is guiding people in increasing their self-awareness, self-management, social awareness, relationship management, identifying their strengths and weaknesses, and identifying the potential that already exists within them. She is guiding people in making positive changes in their life to lead a harmonious, abundant and successful life. Guiding them in BEING THE CHANGE THEY WISH TO SEE...

She is also a contributing author of the No#1 Best Selling Book **"365 Moments of Grace" which was placed No# 1 in 7 categories.** The book launched on 21st June 2016 and is available on Amazon.

She is also a contributing author of the book **"365 Life Shifts: Pivotal Moments That Changed Everything"** releasing in February 2017.

Look forward to her other books, digital products, courses and seminars releasing this year and early next year. ☺

Preface

Namaste

I am grateful to you for picking up this book. In doing so, you have made a decision to take charge of your life and change your destiny. What this indicates is you are ready to design your life and lead a life the way you want to live and not what others decide for you.

Everyone needs motivation and inspiration. No matter whatever you are going through in your life, you must never give up. Develop the habit of reading motivational and inspirational quotes, books, eBooks daily. They always help you to boost your moral and take action. A daily dose of motivation and inspiration is always helpful as it helps you to sail through many situations. It also helps you in achieving the outcomes that you are looking for. When you are motivated and inspired you perform better and are able to take better decisions. Motivation leads to an optimistic and challenging attitude towards life.

This book is really close to my heart because it has an amazing collection of my quotes. There are 365 quotes in this book – one quote for each day to motivate and inspire you. I am sure these heartfelt quotes will definitely help you in transforming your life in various areas. I am sure you will take appropriate actions and keep the forward movement on. Action is the key to success.

I hope this book will help you in taking your personal evolution journey to the next level. Please do write to me, email me, visit our website, and blog. I would be glad to hear from you.

I wish you abundance of great health, wealth, prosperity and success in all areas of your life.

Pooja Shende

Email:- contactus@lotussoul9.com
Website:- www.lotussoul9.com

January 1

Another new day, another new year, another new beginning and another chance to move forward in life. When you sit back and look at the movie of your life, how would you want it to look like? Start producing that movie now. It is never too late. Make it the best movie ever produced and directed. Happy New Year…!

January 2

Don't let your emotions drive you crazy.
Always be crazy enough to be in
the emotion you like to be.

January 3

Don't waste time living in the past striving for things that will give you happiness. Happiness is not an object that once you achieve it will make you feel good. Happiness is a state that you can go into and create it whenever you want. Slip into it now.

January 4

You can be in the right place at the right time. But you have to be the right person in the right place at the right time to succeed.

January 5

See your failures as blessings. It is because of them, you have a great story to share.

January 6

The biggest destroyer of our life is our own EGO. Take out the "E". We are our own biggest enemies. Take the "G" and go beyond your limiting beliefs to create the magic in your life. Take the "O" and obey what your soul says.

January 7

Understanding that the best relationships
are based on understanding and loving each
other is important to understand.

January 8

You don't become an expert in one go. You didn't
learn to ride the cycle in one go and become a gold
medallist. You didn't learn to drive the car in one go
and become a car racer. You didn't learn to cook in
one go and become a master chef. It is over a period
of time with practice and practice and practice you
managed to polish your skills. It is only when you
are working on your skills you achieve mastery.

January 9

When you have a burning desire to fulfil your dreams attached to an organized plan with action and consistency being the driving force behind it, you are bound to make all your dreams come true.

January 10

It is only when we suffer we look inside us.
We become more reflective than ever before.
Reflection is the best tool available with us.
Use it often even in good times.

January 11

Learn to love more and fear less. In doing so,
you start focusing more on the good. Your results
will depend upon what you are focusing on.

January 12

We were born to be real and not perfect.
Chasing perfection is a good thing to do
but chasing your dreams is better.
Making your dreams real by living your
dreams is the ultimate thing to do.

January 13

You can be the change you wish to be
only when you take action.
Action is the key to success.

January 14

The secret to success is to focus on
building the new and not the past.

January 15

Once you overcome your limiting beliefs there will be nothing that would hold you back.

January 16

You are the only one who can take the journey within you.

January 17

Progress is possible only because of change.

January 18

It is when you work on your inner self
you get a shining outer self.

January 19

Leaders become great not just because of their ability to empower themselves, but because of their ability to empower others too.

January 20

When you look at each day as fresh, new and exciting, you would have automatically shed all the limits within you. Be open and receptive to all the good that life is offering you.

January 21

Life is all about memories. Don't wait
for them to happen. Create them.

January 22

Those who cannot change their mind
cannot change anything.

January 23

When you have unlimited choices in life to live your dreams, why restrict yourself to one?

January 24

Creativity is the solution to any challenge that you face. Maintaining your originality using creativity you can overcome anything.

January 25

While you are here in this universe, all the
teachings that you come across are not just to
brighten your day but to transform your life.
Make the most of it now.

January 26

Freedom is the life line of the soul.

January 27

Each moment is filled with joy and happiness;
it is just that you need to focus there.

January 28

Your physical world is the output of
what you create inside you.

January 29

To remain stuck in a situation or
come out of it is your choice.
Choose wisely.

January 30

A true friend accepts you the way you are but
also helps you to be the change you wish to be.

January 31

There is growth on the other side of fear.

February 1

In order to be wealthy you need to first believe that you can be wealthy. You need to believe that you deserve wealth.

February 2

Each one of us is unique and we are here to make a contribution to the Universe.

February 3

The state of your mind will lead to the state of your emotions. Your state of your emotions will lead you to certain actions which in turn produce certain results. If you want improved results, improve the state of your mind.

February 4

Make time to do the things that your soul loves to do.

February 5

Whenever you fall, you must get up.
The fall is like poison.
Don't allow it to enter your life.

February 6

Having butterflies in your stomach just means
that you are moving closer to growth.

February 7

Believe you can do it and you will.

February 8

You are responsible for your life.
Be responsible today and every day.

February 9

Don't bother when children don't listen
to you. But do bother your behaviour as
children are always watching you.

February 10

Fear is a negative emotion. When your mind is filled with fear, you not only destroy your own intelligence but you also transmit these destructive vibrations to all the people who come in contact with you and their chances too. Face your fears and overcome them now not only for your own good but for the good of everyone.

February 11

Knowing yourself is more important than knowing the outer world. Knowing yourself will lead you to the secrets of the knowing the outer world.

February 12

You cannot change something till the
time you accept the change.

February 13

There is something within us which
already knows everything about us.

February 14

We don't stop playing, laughing, singing, and dancing because we are growing old. We grow old because we stopped playing, laughing, singing and dancing. Keep the child inside you "ALIVE".

February 15

When you arrived in this world, you were empty handed. When you leave this world, you will leave empty handed. Accumulate good karma that is what you can carry with you.

February 16

Forgiving others does not mean that you are weak.
Forgiving others displays the strength you carry.

February 17

Don't get driven away by temporary defeat.
Keep moving forward.
You are born to succeed.

February 18

If you keep believing that you are not good enough it will soon convert into reality. Instead, think of what you want to become so that it becomes the reality.

February 19

If you want your success to last forever then the purpose of doing that act should come from within. If you are trying to achieve something just because someone challenged you or you want to prove a point to someone your success will be short lived.

February 20

When we stop putting ourselves first in our life,
we stop ourselves from being a priority. Put
yourself first today and be the VIP of your life.
VIP = Very Important Person

February 21

Know that your thought and action in
important for you to live in the present
rather than living in the past [unaware].

February 22

The more you run away from your fears, the more they will haunt you. Instead, stay strong and face them. Be brave today.

February 23

Know that you can easily release any unsupportive belief from the past in any area of your life and create a new belief easily that helps you to become what you want to be.

February 24

If you don't go after what you want,
you will never have it.
Go for it now.

February 25

Doing one thing every day that makes you
feel happy will increase yours and others
happiness quotient too. Lead by example.

February 26

It's not about how you fell down.
It's about how and what you did to get back on your feet.

February 27

It's ok, if people don't understand you.
It's more important for you to understand yourself.

February 28

Each thought of yours will either empower you
or disempower you. Each thought of yours will
either take you towards success or unhappiness.
Choose your thoughts carefully and wisely.

March 1

At times, you are not your beliefs. The beliefs
might have been passed on to you from generations
together. Talk to yourself often and find out what
are the beliefs that are taking you towards success.
If they are not moving you towards success it
is high time for you to release them and make
room for new ones. The ones you believe in.

March 2

You are never too late, never too young,
and never too old to dream. Only when you
dream, you can make them come true.
Think big and beyond. The time is now.

March 3

Blaming others for not being successful will
not take you anywhere. Point to yourself and
see what is it that you need to change.

March 4

Don't worry if some people don't like you. There are some people who still don't like and love themselves.

March 5

If you don't want to be categorized as a complainer then stop complaining. At the same time ensure that you are not in the company of complainers.

March 6

There are no failures – they are experiences.
These experiences fuel my passion
and make it stronger every day.
Never give up.

March 7

Be in the present, feel the present, breathe the present.
Be present today.

March 8

To experience life you don't have to go to a university. Look at your own life experiences. That itself is a big university of amazing learnings.

March 9

Mediocre performers use these excuses; that's not possible, I can't do it, it's a waste of time, no point trying it out, we will be back to square one. Successful performers don't use this language. They go opposite. They say; everything is possible, I can do it, it is an investment, I just did that, I am at the top.

March 10

If you are constantly seeking attention, it is
impossible for you to be happy and successful.

March 11

Travel and explore the world.
Your experiences will never be the same.

March 12

Think of solutions which are beyond
your current capacity to create.
It is then that you learn and grow.

March 13

A dream, a burning desire and a definite plan are
the greatest means for fulfilling your dream.

March 14

Success is not a destination; it's about the journey.

March 15

Success would be –
Making an impact bigger and beyond your goals.

March 16

Small thinking leads to small actions. Think
big and beyond if you want bigger results.

March 17

Do the things that you don't like
first, and get rid of them.
Keep it simple.

March 18

If you are not working towards making your dreams to come true then someone else will make you work towards making their dreams come true. Choice is yours.

March 19

Life will keep presenting a lot of twist, turns and straight roads too. Enjoy each one. Each one has its own charm and story. You never know what it will lead you to.

March 20

Hold no place for people who do not
want you to grow in your life.
Clear that place to hold people who want you to grow.

March 21

Create a life that looks and feels good inside and outside.

March 22

Put your mind, heart and soul when
working on your dreams.
That's the secret to making you dreams come true.

March 23

Those who know me don't doubt me.
They just believe in me and follow me.

March 24

You will succeed only when you
believe you can succeed.
Believing in yourself is the key to success.

March 25

Don't wait for a weekend to indulge in doing
what you love to do. Live, breathe and work
towards your dreams every single day.
Live your dreams.

March 26

Don't go after proving people wrong
and proving that you are correct.
Go after the result that you want to see.

March 27

Every year when you look back at life,
you should be able to say –
"I lived the life that I wanted to live".

March 28

Don't be afraid to start all over again.
It's another chance to achieve what you want in life.

March 29

Don't wait for opportunities to
come and knock your door.
Create opportunities instead.

March 30

Be thankful for all the love, joy, abundance
and all the good in your life. If you focus
on it, you will find it everywhere.

March 31

Pay close attention to the first reaction of yours in any
situation. It sets the tone for handling the situation. If
you feel it is not taking you towards success, change it.

April 1

Focusing too much on your weakness and ignoring your strength - one day will convert your strength into weakness. Instead, convert your weakness into strength and work on polishing your strength further.

April 2

Choosing is better than wanting something. But committing yourself to something that you want is the best option.

April 3

Keep working towards your goals. Never give up. You never know, the next moment might be the turning point of your life.

April 4

Every moment of your life has the potential of becoming the greatest moment of your life. Celebrate life.

April 5

A beautiful body will age one day but a beautiful soul will continue to remain a beautiful soul.

April 6

I don't know who is on this journey of life with me. All I know is - "I am with myself on this wonderful journey of life."

April 7

Have no expectations from others. Help people,
even when you know they can't help you in return
for those are the times they need you most.

April 8

Surround yourself with people who motivate you,
inspire you, encourage you, and believe in your dreams
for they are ones who are not only on the journey of
life with you but are also pushing you forward.

April 9

Don't listen to people who put you down.
They are the ones who never succeeded.

April 10

Keep your desire for success so strong that
the fear of failure just melts away.

April 11

Don't think about what could go wrong.
Instead, think about what could go right.

April 12

Making a big life change might be scary.
You know what? Not making that change is
scarier. Be the change that you wish to be.

April 13

Keep moving ahead. It's shaping you to become the best, for your best.

April 14

Smile is the only thing that can make you look attractive.
Keep smiling.

April 15

Don't follow the footprints of others.
Create your own footprints.

April 16

Believe that you are worthy of having
abundance in your life and your good comes
from everywhere and everyone.

April 17

Don't predict your future. Create it.
It is always bright when you create it.

April 18

As we let our light shine, we brighten the life of people
we connect with. Not only are they motivated to do so
but also keep the light on for generations to come.

April 19

All the answers to the questions that you
are searching for are within you. Reflection
is the best tool you have with you.
The Power is within you.

April 20

Sometimes you fall down in life because the
answers to the direction you need to take are
hidden there. Embrace your fall, reflect and
think of ways to move ahead.

April 21

Everyone has a genius inside them. It is just that you need to believe and get it out. Be iconic today.

April 22

Get away with the fear of death. Everyone has to leave this body someday. You can't escape it. Instead, accept this and tell yourself that whatever time you are here you are going to make the best of it. Live life to fullest and make it a memorable journey so that when you are on the death bed you are content with your life.

April 23

Leave footprints of love, kindness, respect and gratitude.

April 24

Every time you breathe, you get a chance to change.
Live your life now.

April 25

For things to change, I have to change. For things to get better, I have to get better. I am designing my new story now. Are you?

April 26

I am not my emotion.
I choose the emotion I want to be in.

April 27

Is your focus on obstacles or opportunities? Is the focus on risk or rewards? This will determine whether you will be successful or not. Take charge of your life now. The power is within you.

April 28

I believe in myself.
Miracles happen to me all the time.

April 29

If you want to experience something,
the best thing is to get into action.

April 30

Whenever failure strikes you, get up and fight back.
Don't allow it to hamper your spirit.
Never give up.

May 1

I have known hardships, I have been broken, and I have missed my targets. But I still stand tall moving ahead and building bridges over the gaps. Every step that I take makes me stronger and happier. It gets me closer to my higher purpose of life.

May 2

There are no problems. They are opportunities that life gives you to start walking on the path to success.

May 3

Every step that you take brings you closer to your goals.

May 4

Passion is the main ingredient of your goals. Passion is the driving force behind your goals. Be passionate now.

May 5

If you have not spoken, you are not heard. If you do not promote, you cannot sell. If you do not breathe, you cannot live. Action is the key to success.

May 6

Loving yourself does not mean that you are selfish. Instead it makes you a more lovable person.

May 7

The secret to success is not to run away from your problems. The secret is to make such a bigger impact that your problems do not remain as problems any more.

May 8

In difficult times, you come to know more about your strengths and your weakness. In difficult times, you also come to know who your greatest friends truly are. Lessons learnt from the difficult times are the best lessons learnt ever.

May 9

I am unstoppable. My own strength inspires me.
I am courageous.

May 10

Tough times never last but tough people do.
Don't search for tough people.
You are one of them. Be courageous today.

May 11

Good friends make good times better and the bad times easier. They are the ones who understand how important it is to support and be with each other.

May 12

When you open your arms and tell the Universe that you love, value, respect and support yourself and everyone, in turn you will receive love, value, respect and support from the Universe.

May 13

Be patient and sincere with yourself. This is what will definitely help you achieve your goals.

May 14

In this journey of life, you will have to cross over many pit falls. At times there might be people who throw stones at you. It's like a splash of muddy water with some pebbles on your windscreen while driving. Be your own wiper and clear them off. Get the focus back on the journey of life. Welcome and accept the adventure in your life with grace. Life is a beautiful journey. Happy Journey!

May 15

Why complicate life when you can keep it simple?

May 16

Beliefs are the most important part of your soul. For your soul to feel self-fulfilling, your beliefs need to make things happen.

May 17

Staying fit mentally, emotionally and physically is not a destination. It is a way of life. Set your lifestyle now!

May 18

You are the most powerful magnet for success. You contain everything and anything that is required to be successful. Realise the power of your thoughts now and use them effectively.

May 19

It's all about "fitness".
Fit mind, fit body, fit soul, makes a fit you.

May 20

There is no fun in laughing on others. It is more fun
when you look back and laugh at yourself. Be Happy!

May 21

———

An athlete always pushes the feet back to get the jump start in the race. An arrow is always pulled backward before shooting it. Remember, when life pulls you back (so called difficult times) – it is preparing to launch you to achieve something greater in life.

May 22

———

The real purpose of running your own race is just not to win but to get the best out of you when you push your limits. Run your race now!

May 23

Running away from the problem is not going to provide you a solution. Instead - face it!

May 24

Don't just tell your life what to do. Listen to it as well to understand what it wants you to do.

May 25

Believe that something wonderful is always
happening with you and it will happen.

May 26

7 things money can't buy:
Love
Time
Family
Respect
Passion
Happiness
Inner peace

May 27

Be generous with yourself, for you are the
only one in your mind. You are the only one
in your soul and body. Love yourself beyond
imagination and see how things change for you.

May 28

The secret to success is a team work of your
heart, mind and soul working towards it.

May 29

When no one believed in me, I believed
in myself even more. I am glad, I did that.
That has made me what I am today.

May 30

Just breathe, have faith, believe in
yourself, be optimistic.
Miracles do happen.

May 31

The challenge is not in learning new habits,
but in unlearning the bad ones.

June 1

When you start to unlearn your negative thoughts,
your positive vibrations will automatically increase.
It is then that life welcomes you with open arms.

June 2

Your life is in your hands. Paint the most beautiful and colourful life beyond imagination. Add the most melodious music beyond creation. Add the most beautiful of the expressions you could ever give to it. Be the artist of your life. The time is now.

June 3

If you are waiting to create wealth through an easy way, you will remain broke life long. But if you are willing to do whatever it takes to create wealth, you are a success.

June 4

You can shape your future only if you believe in it.

June 5

Personal development is not about making you feel helpless. It's about helping you not to become helpless. Work on developing yourself now.

June 6

Life is a beautiful journey with amazing adventures.
Happy Journey!

June 7

Smile, you are on camera.
Don't forget, he (God) is always watching you.

June 8

Don't let the darkness of the sky
(problems) fade you out.
Be the light. Be the one to light the lamp
in yours and other people's life.

June 9

There is nothing as hopeless or useless.
You have the power to change every single
moment of your life. Act now.

June 10

The best gift you can give your family is your time. Soon, children will grow up and get busy making their own life. Click as many pictures in your memory and your camera of these sweet moments for you to always look back and feel happy about. Make time for your family now!

June 11

If you feel good about yourself, you will produce good results. If you feel stale about yourself, you will produce stale results.

June 12

In your journey of life when you are trying to reach your full potential, help others to reach their full potential too. You never know who needs whom and when!

June 13

The power is within you. Act now!

June 14

You have a mind. Control it.
Do what you want to do and not
what others want you to do.

June 15

Carry a winning attitude but when you
win ensure to express gratitude.
It will always help you to stay grounded
and focused on your next goal.
Expressing gratitude is the greatest thing to do.

June 16

The book you are reading now
reflects your state of mind.
The book you are writing now
reflects your quest for life.

June 17

Every moment is an important moment of our
life. Every moment is a successful moment of our
life. It depends on how you look at it and think
about it. That is what creates your reality.

June 18

Speak about your blessings more and not the
problems that you are facing. Spread love and
not hatred. Be optimistic and not negative in
every situation you go through in life.
Welcome the good in your life now!

June 19

Every day bow to the divine in you.
Be thankful for what you have.
At the same time forgive yourself for
anything that is hurting you.
No one is perfect and so are you.

June 20

No matter what, get up and dress up well every day. It's not about presenting yourself well in front of others. It's about making you feel good about yourself every moment, every hour, and every day. Be cheerful today and every day.

June 21

Life is a beautiful and colourful journey. Using appropriate colours can make it look gloomy or bright. Choose your colours wisely.

June 22

It's not about life. It's about "YOU".
YOU and only YOU can make the
difference in yours and others life.
Be special today and every day.

June 23

Negative people focus on the ugly side of their life.
Positive people focus on the good in their life.
Focus on the good now.

June 24

There are no hard, difficult or tough times.
When you get any of these feelings, remember
it is the best time to get the best out of you.
Be brave today and every day.

June 25

I am unique. I am different.
I love it this way.

June 26

When everything seems to be going wrong, remember;
something great is coming your way soon. It's just
another way to clear the old and bring in the new.

June 27

For a bird to come to life and fly, it is important
for the shell to break. Similarly, if you have
to succeed, you have to come out of your
shell and overcome your limiting beliefs.
Life is waiting for you to fly.

June 28

Break the shackles.
Don't get dragged away by what people tag you with.
Don't lose sleep over what you are not.
Focus on being iconic.
Be iconic today!

June 29

You were born successful. Then why doubt it.
Start believing in yourself and keep
the forward movement on.

June 30

Our children are the architects of future. Many a times we don't trust them and don't give them the freedom to choose what they want to be. Let them go in the direction that they want to go. They might be building a better future than you thought for them. Let them be the change they wish to be.

July 1

Just as the lotus flower blossoms out from the mud, never give up in life. Whatever the circumstances might be! They are there to make you blossom like a lotus. Be a lotus now.

July 2

Seize the moment. Live in the present.
Be present today.

July 3

Life moves on. No two moments are the same.
Keep the forward movement on.
Celebrate life.

July 4

Either you take charge of your life
or life takes charge of you.
Take charge of yourself. The power is within you.

July 5

You are your own obstacle. Live the life of your dreams.

July 6

You already have what it takes to be successful. You just need to keep polishing it. You are "Success"!

July 7

Treat people well.
You never know what they are going through.
You will either make them or break them.
Choice is yours.

July 8

You can fail at what you are asked to do.
But you can never fail at doing what you love to do.

July 9

Don't rely on others opinion about your
capabilities and weakness. Instead boost
your abilities through self-reflection.
This is the tool which is always there with you.

July 10

Don't allow any situation to break you.
Instead use it to make "you".

July 11

Don't look outside. Look inside.
Be your own best friend.

July 12

Critics will always criticize, that's their job. Your
job is to make your dream come true. Don't
allow the critics to take control of your life.
The Power is within you. Chase your dreams now.

July 13

People might not listen to you but they
are always observing you.
Lead by example.

July 14

Hardships in life don't make you weak.
They make you even stronger.
Don't run away from them. Face them.

July 15

Do you want to be a shadow of someone
else or you want to be what you want to
be. Be your original self today.

July 16

In order to see the change: -
You need to be the change that you wish to see.

July 17

Imagine work and life as the two tyres of a bicycle.
As a pedal is required to keep the bicycle moving
ahead, understanding, cooperation and a rhythm
is required between work and life to keep the
forward movement on. Be the pedal today.

July 18

Inspiration and motivation are like fuel.
Using it to ignite the soul will help you
achieve things beyond your imagination.

July 19

There is no shortcut to success other
than working towards it.

July 20

Team work can only happen when the
focus is on "We" and not "I".

July 21

There is only one success mantra:-
"Don't lose focus of your goal."

July 22

The way you start your day, sets the frequency
for the day. Take charge of yourself. Tune
into the right station frequency now.

July 23

Don't ever compare yourself with anyone.
Analyse your past and present results
to produce a better future.

July 24

There might be certain delays in achieving your goal but keep working towards it. Eventually you will succeed.

July 25

You have been gifted a beautiful life.
It is up to you to open the gift or keep it aside.

July 26

I am fuelled by passion and driven by faith.
What about you?

July 27

Being the light in someone's life makes you and
they shine brighter and brighter. Be the light.

July 28

When you work in harmony with yourself for a definite objective you put yourself in a position of power house, you are bound to succeed.

July 29

A failure is not a failure when you move ahead.
It is lessons learned.

July 30

You have to let go your past to become the future.
For that you need to act today.

July 31

Don't allow anyone to take away your peace of mind.

August 1

Don't allow your mind to rust. Read for a minimum
of 20 minutes daily and prevent it from rusting.
After all, Prevention is better than cure.

August 2

Don't underestimate the power of your mind.
It can achieve things beyond your imagination.

August 3

The best gift you can give yourself
is believing in yourself.

August 4

Don't focus on the past and cry over it.
Instead focus on the beautiful learning it has
given you. Focus on the good in life.

August 5

Always smile at each and every
challenge you face in life.
It will no longer be a challenge.

August 6

Whenever you are tired, just relax. That is the best
gift you can give your mind, body and soul.

August 7

For being successful, you don't need
to wait for opportunities.
You need to create "The Opportunity".

August 8

Always keep your mind filled with
optimistic and powerful thoughts.
Leave no room for the negatives.

August 9

Flying high is not bad but is depends
on where you are flying -
above or below the clouds!

August 10

Meditation is one of the most important
and powerful ingredient to living a happy,
peaceful and successful life.

August 11

Be so good at what you do that it makes
your challenge look smaller.

August 12

Be so good at what you do that it tempts
people to acknowledge you.

August 13

Don't make people fall in love with who you are not.
Make them fall in love with who you are.

August 14

No one can make your dreams come true.
You will have to do it yourself.

August 15

Every day prayers are like charging your own batteries.
Believe in the power of prayers with action
attached to it. It does create miracles.

August 16

Like bathing, cleansing of your
mind is required every day.

August 17

We are so busy in presenting ourselves to the
world that we forget who we truly are.

August 18

The reason ordinary people become extra-ordinary is
because they never give up. Be extra-ordinary now.

August 19

Don't just read other people's success story!
Start writing your success story now.

August 20

Time never waits for anyone. What you are waiting for?
You and only you can get the change in your life.

August 21

For something to grow, you need to plant
the seed first. Plant the seed of
abundance, joy, happiness, love, prosperity,
courage, confidence, bliss, freedom,
zest and intelligence now.

August 22

Team work between mind, body and soul
helps you conquer any situation.

August 23

(-) the negatives (+) the positives
Life is a beautiful and colourful journey.

August 24

Every picture tells a story.
To make it beautiful or ugly is your choice.

August 25

You are your own jewel.
Look inside. You already have
everything that it takes to excel.

August 26

You cannot become successful without
the lessons learnt from failure.
They are equally important!

August 27

If you do not have any dreams, you have no vision.
When you do not have a vision, you
do not have any mission.
When you do not have any mission, you
do not have any goals in life.
When you do not have any goals in
life, you have not lived life.
You are dead!
Be alive today. Live life! Think big and beyond
Rise and shine forever.

August 28

Be the Rainbow in someone else's life as well as yours.

R - recharge
A - appreciate
I - inner
N - nest
B - before
O - over
W - worked

August 29

Everyone talks about building relationships
with your customer, your team, your family. But
how is your relationship with yourself? To build
relationships with others, first build a relationship
with yourself. Be your own best friend.

August 30

You are not fully dressed until you wear your smile.
Keep smiling.

August 31

Sometimes the solution is not in
doing the difficult things.
It is in doing the simple things.

September 1

Sometimes it's good to slow down in life.
Relax, take stock of your life and bounce back.

September 2

Only when you overcome your fears, will you
be able to teach people how to do that.

September 3

You don't have to explain yourself every time.
Those who understand you don't
need it and will not ask for it.

September 4

One smile can change the entire situation. Keep smiling.

September 5

We always know what we want to be and what we want to do. It is just that we do not look for the answers which are hidden within us.

September 6

Trust that everything happens in the perfect time,
space and sequence. Just flow in the process
and everything will start falling in place.

September 7

Smile often. It's not only good for you but
you never know who needs your smile.

September 8

When you keep walking in the direction of your fears, you will soon overcome them. When you overcome them, they will serve as an eye opener to make the mission of life much bigger and beyond imagination.

September 9

Don't try to control your destiny. Instead, create it by making the choices you want to make.

September 10

Control your mind by keeping it busy to work towards
your purpose of life by following a definite plan.

September 11

On this journey of life, you will come
across many challenging situations. It is up
to you to face them or break down.

September 12

Don't waste time planning for things without
a vision and mission. Instead ask yourself:
"What is your vision and mission in life?"
"What is it that you love doing?"
"What is it that you are passionate about?"
"What things are important for you?"
"What standards will you follow in living your life?"
"If you have to live your dreams, what actions
are required to fulfil those dreams?"
"What is it that you want to become as
a result of the actions you take?"

September 13

You are not your parents, your friends or relatives.
You are your own unique self. You are a capable person.
The power is within you.

September 14

If you are not clear of where you want to go, then
how will you know that the opportunity standing
in front of you is the right choice for you.
First, gain clarity about what where
you want to be in life.

September 15

Stop comparing yourself with others. Study
the life of successful people and you will find
that they too had flaws in them. But they never
bothered about who thinks what about them.
They were on a mission to be the
change they wanted to be.

September 16

So what if no one is on the journey of life
with you. It is important for you to be on
this journey of life with yourselves.
Trust yourself and be the driving force for yourself.

September 17

Every day spend few hours alone doing the
things that you love to do the most. Otherwise
the day will take these hours from you, making
you do the things it wants you to do.

September 18

There is no right or wrong. There is nothing that is perfect or imperfect. It depends on the person's perception about the situation. Something may be right for them. It might not be for you. Something might be perfect for them. It might not be for you. You don't have to follow people's perception about the situation. Do what you feel is right for you.

September 19

Stop being so busy that you do not have the time to evaluate yourself. If you want to lead a successful life, you will have to keep evaluate yourself regularly and the life that you are living.

September 20

Once you start living the life that you have designed for yourself, you have decided upon the values that are important for you, the people who you want on this journey of life, the surroundings that you want to be in, the choices that you want to make – all this will determine the journey that you will be walking on for the rest of your life.

September 21

Once you have embarked on the journey of self-development and self-awareness, you will realise that many of the concepts or ideas that you believed in, some people whom you believed in might not hold any good now. Just let them go. Once you learn to let go, you start walking on the path to being closer to your own self.

September 22

Knowing others is not as important as knowing yourself.
Human body is amazingly intelligent. It keeps
giving us signals of what is happening inside us.
But we are so busy being busy that we do not tend
to listen or ignore these signals. This is when we
stop interacting with ourselves and invite trouble.
Listen to your body now.

September 23

We have been gifted with great gifts. Instead
for searching for them within us, we search
and expect them from the materialistic world.
Look within yourself. You are priceless.

September 24

The more you talk to yourself, the clearer your vision and mission in life will be. The better you will be able to lead your life. Reflection is the best tool. It is within you. Make use of it now.

September 25

If you observe your wounds closely, you will realise they were the stepping stones to success.

September 26

Before a victory, a person must have experienced defeat many times. The key to victory is to keep the focus on, keep working towards it and never give up.

September 27

Sufferings in life are not punishments. They are indication of you moving towards a stronger and greater you.

September 28

Nobody likes to suffer. Ever realised that it is because of them, we open up, look inside ourselves, search for answers to the questions we are looking for, fight back to get stronger and a better person.

September 29

Only when we experience the four seasons, we come to know what it feels like in summer, winter, autumn and spring. It is then we get to enjoy everything what nature has in store for us and we look forward to it. Similarly in life, only when we face various challenges that life has in store for us, we look forward to love, happiness, and joy.

September 30

Conflict in your mind is not always bad. The free flow of conflicting ideas helps you to come out with creative solutions that you might not have thought of them otherwise. You can pick up the best solution then.

October 1

Only when you are not scared of
failure, you will succeed.
None can insult you without your permission.
Don't give others the right to control your life. Take charge of your life now. The power is within you.

October 2

On the journey of becoming a better you, enjoy the challenges that life presents in front of you. When you treat these challenges as experiences, you will realise that you are better equipped and are able to sail through easily.

October 3

The view of the mountains from the valley is awesome. The view of the valley from the mountain top is awesome too. In life, at times you might be feeling a bit low. At times, you might be at your highest peak. But the learnings from both the points are important or else you will not know what your weakness and strengths are.

October 4

If you do not love yourself enough, you are restricting
yourself from trusting life. If you do not trust life,
how will you be able to lead a successful life?
Put yourself first and lead by example.

October 5

Be the one who takes action and not the one who is
sitting on the bench criticising and complaining.

October 6

You cannot shape your future if you didn't
believe that you have a future.

October 7

It's your job as the leader of your life to create
situations that you want rather than to surrender
to the situations that you don't want.

October 8

Just because your path is spiral does not mean that it will not lead you to success. The path to success is not always straight.

October 9

To make a living is important. But what is more important is does it make your life too.

October 10

Don't just restrict and limit happiness to making yourself feel happy. When you spread happiness it multiplies beyond imagination. Spread happiness now.

October 11

The person you are going to spend the most time with is your own self. So why not be your own best friend? Be the most loving, caring and supportive person you ever know. Be the fittest person you ever know. Be the best support system you ever know.

October 12

You are never too late for doing what you want to do in life. The day you realise this, that is the opening of another path for you to walk on.

October 13

Always remember you are UNIQUE. Even if two people have similar features, skin colour, hair and tone – they will never have the same experiences of life.

October 14

Gaining clarity about the purpose of your
life simplifies your journey of life.

October 15

There might be many things that you must have
experienced in the past. There might be many things
that you want to experience in the future. And there
are also a lot of things going inside us. When you
get that out into the world, you will experience
miracles. Miracles do happen. Believe in yourself.

October 16

Don't just restrict your knowledge and wisdom to what
your parents, teachers or other people have exposed
you to. Look within yourself. You will realise there
is a wealth of knowledge and wisdom inside you.

October 17

Keep your eyes on reaching the stars and the
moon. But always keep your feet grounded deep
inside for never to lose track of your dreams.

October 18

Don't preserve resources with a mind-set that there is going to be scarcity of them soon. Preserve resources with the mind-set that there is abundance and your actions are helping in multiplying the abundance.

October 19

Respect the courageous. It takes a lot of courage for people to be courageous.

October 20

Courage always necessarily does not mean that you stand up and speak. It takes courage to listen to a trauma victim and still be there with them to empower them.

October 21

Till the time you do not take action on the words of wisdom that you are receiving, it is equivalent to none for you.

October 22

No Risk, No Pain = No Gain
Till the time you are not willing to step out
of your zone and take action, you will not be
able to achieve what you want to achieve.

October 23

Faith is to believe in what you are not able to see now
and it comes as a reward when it actually happens.

October 24

Be the light. Don't depend too much on others.
In darkness, even your shadow leaves you alone.
Make yourself so strong that even in difficult
times your own light lights up the path for you.

October 25

The more you encourage yourself to accept
your imperfections and faults, the better
prepared and composed you are to work on
them and move towards a better you.

October 26

If you are able to experience and feel joy that means you know how it felt when you experienced sadness, grief and sorrow. It is important for us to accept and experience both the emotions otherwise we cannot judge what joy or sorrow means to us.

October 27

We fear about something not because of the fear of experiencing it but because we have not seen ourselves doing it. When we go through it we know that there will be no fear next time and you can keep doing it successfully.

October 28

When you discover what is right and purposeful for you, you will automatically start walking on that path. The necessary resources required for you to walk on that path will automatically appear in front of you. Focus on where you want to be in life. Rest will follow through.

October 29

The problem is not "out there". It is within us.
The solution is not "out there". It is within us.

October 30

Give the best to the world from the bottom of
your heart and soul. In doing so, you receive the
best from the world which touches your heart and
soul. Success or failure will not matter then.

October 31

You can buy the services and offerings of people
but you cannot buy the heart that beats inside
them. You cannot buy the love that spreads from
their heart. You cannot buy the respect that
comes from within them. You have to earn it.

November 1

Learn to respect other people's opinion and thought process if you want them to respect your opinion.

November 2

Gratitude is a powerful process by which you not only thank and feel grateful for what you have in life but also attract more good in doing so.

November 3

No one can experience fear the way fear means to you except you. Similarly no one can experience courage and strength the way you built your courage and strength except you. The power is within you.

November 4

Procrastination is the best way to delay your success. Action is the only way to speed up your success.

November 5

There is no hope of success for a person
who does not want to get ahead in life.

November 6

Focus on self-mastery first then on the
outside world. If you do not conquer yourself
someone else will conquer you soon.

November 7

Self-mastery does not just focus on controlling
your thoughts. It focuses on all aspects of
your life mental, physical and emotional.

November 8

Consistency is required to stay tuned on your path
to success. Always finish what you have started.
Set smaller milestones to stay focused and celebrate
every milestone that you achieve. Giving up in
between is the first sign of failure. Never give up.

November 9

You will never be successful if you are working with a negative mind set on the purpose or goals in life. Stop playing small. Be optimistic today.

November 10

If you are always in a dilemma, you can never take decisions. Either you are clear about the scenario or unclear about it.

November 11

Master your fears before your fears master over you.
Unless you have a harmonious relationship
with yourself, failure is there to follow you in
terms of unhappiness, losing sight of your vision
and mission, or disturbed relationship with
others and much more. In order to be a success
improve your relationship with yourself.

November 12

Keeping an open mind and being afraid of nothing
converts impossible to possible. What are you
afraid of then? Make the impossible possible.

November 13

The most important step to success is to choose
and work towards what you want to achieve
and not what others want to achieve.

November 14

Focusing on too many things will not take you
anywhere. Focus on one thing that is important to take
your milestone to the next level. It will automatically
open the gates for many more milestones.

November 15

Save money with a prosperity mind-set of having abundance in life now and always. Saving money with a fearful mind-set will scale down your happiness quotient of having abundance in your life.

November 16

If you are not enthusiastic and passionate about your purpose and goals in life, you are not enjoying the journey of what you are in the process of becoming.

November 17

Searching for solutions with a closed mind-set will not lead you anywhere rather will land up in more problematic situations. An open mind-set is the key to working in a solutions mode.

November 18

True leader carries his people along with him and not just make them follow him. It is up to the people to follow him.

November 19

Power when gifted to you makes you feel successful and powerful but soon starts evaporating if you fail to realise that the real power is within you.

November 20

I am busy chasing my dream. I am
busy living my dream.
I am unstoppable.

November 21

You don't need permission from anyone to be what you want to be. Other than you no one else can give you the right to be what you want to be. What are you waiting for?

November 22

Only when you have lost someone close, you realise that they were precious gifts in your life. Why wait to lose, rather live to cherish!

November 23

Willingness to do something and actually doing something are two different things. Willingness will help you to come in a state to move towards your higher purpose in life. Taking actions will actually help you achieve the higher purpose.

November 24

I am unstoppable. I am a magnet of success. I am busy living my dream. I am courageous. I am powerful. I am confident. I am loveable. I am thankful for all the love in my life. I am creating happy and joyful memories every moment. I am in harmony with myself. I am worthy of having abundance in my life. I am success.

November 25

Habit is a culture that you develop in yourself. It's your choice to have good or bad habits installed in you. This will determine what type of culture you are building for yourself and the next generations to come.

November 26

Even if your plan is not accurate but is an organized plan which mentions a step by step approach, you can always fine tune it. But functioning without a plan is like searching for the direction and path that you need to walk on.

November 27

Taking regular breaks in a planned way from
your routine will not only make you feel
good but also empower you to perform better.
Before the situation breaks you down, take
a break to break down the situation.

November 28

When you are committed to achieve what
you want, the doors to make it happen
will automatically start opening.

November 29

Shutting the door to negative influences or negative
people is the key to developing consistency
in your action on the path to success.

November 30

The sound of the voice speaking from within
is more soother than the nightingale singing.
Always make time to listen to your inner voice.

December 1

It is not necessary that in order to aim for higher goals or purpose in life you have to take bigger and larger steps. Sometimes a small change can lead to a larger impact.

December 2

Once you have mastered a skill you can never be called a beginner. But once upon a time you were a beginner. The lesson learnt in the journey from a beginner to a master is what makes you a master. Being a beginner or a master is not important. It is the journey that plays an important role.

December 3

You are not anybody. You are your own unique self.

December 4

A dream, a burning desire and a definite plan are
the greatest means for fulfilling your dream.

December 5

If you do not raise your bar, define the framework and standards that you want to follow in life to achieve your higher purpose of life, then, you will keep yourself starving from what you deserve in life.

December 6

Staying calm, composed and silent even after knowing the fact that people are talking behind your back - displays your strength and composure.
You have better things to do rather than focusing on the negativity.
Stay tall. Focus on the good in life.

December 7

Lack of clarity, doubt and fear can be overcome by taking action. But what type of action you are taking is the key to overcoming them. If you get driven by fear and become more fearful it will not lead you anywhere. To overcome fear, you have to move towards your fear and not run away from it.

December 8

Bring out the treasures hidden within you. The time is now.

December 9

Get away with the habit of worrying. It does not add any value to your life. When you tell yourself that all is well in your world and you are safe, you will realise that with this decision you feel a peace of mind and calmness in your thoughts.

December 10

If you want to enjoy the fruits of abundance then plant the seed of abundance in your life in a way that no one can ever uproot the roots.

December 11

Get away with the fear of poverty and move towards a prosperity mind-set. Tell yourself that there is abundance for you and everyone. The very fact of you breathing and alive today speaks of you being abundant.

December 12

When you continue to hold the negative thoughts within you, soon you are soaked in them and they become a part of your character. Choice is yours, either to replace them with the positive thoughts or continue to hold the negative thoughts.

December 13

You have the power to control your mind. You have the power to feed what you want in your mind. You have the power to create the environment that you want. You have the power to do whatever you wish to be. Choice is yours either you neglect this power or use this power to achieve success. Get Set Go...

December 14

Tolerating negative influences is inviting evils into your life.

December 15

Your brain is like a broad casting and receiving station for thoughts. Use it effectively to get what you want in life.

December 16

It is never too crowded at the top. It is your choice whether you want to be a part of the crowd and feel suffocated or be at the top enjoying the breeze of success.

December 17

Urgent and Important are too different thing. Urgent might not always be important. But important will always be important.

December 18

STOP poisoning your mind and other peoples mind by providing negative suggestions.

December 19

We already have everything that we
need to be what we want to be.
It is just that on the journey of life we get
influenced by the situations, surroundings and
people. In the process we land up surrendering
to them. Instead focus on what you want to be
in life. Your focus will influence the situation,
surrounding and people to work in your favour.

December 20

Move away from the "if then else" scenario
and start being real. Excuses will not take
you anywhere. Your action will.

December 21

In the game of chess, every single move is important. It can change the whole game. Similarly in the game of life, every single thought is important. It has the power to change the results of life. Think wisely.

December 22

Be willing to let go some of your old patterns of thinking and adopt the new ones. Only when you let go you create space for the new ones.

December 23

What's the point in having the right tools
that you need to become what you want
to be if you are not using them?

December 24

You and only you can get the winds
of change in your life.

December 25

Your beliefs, your thinking and your character determines the level of your success. Keep upgrading them if you want to reach higher in life.

December 26

What you cannot see is more powerful than that you can see. No one might notice the effort that goes behind becoming successful. It is the effort and the steps that you took which made you successful.

December 27

Even if you have acquired enough wealth
but you are not ready from inside there are
always chances of you losing it. Be prepared
for wealth if you want wealth in your life.

December 28

It's just not enough to have the right tools
in place to help you move forward if you
are not willing to move forward.

December 29

You are a possessor of greatness.
The invisible creates the visible. Build your character
in a way that your persona attracts what you want.

December 30

Lack of money is merely a mind-set reflecting
your inner world. Change the inner world
if you want to change the outer world.

December 31

A seed turns into a plant and then into a tree. It then starts to blossom with flowers, fruits and gives us shade too. Similarly, when you bow the seed of abundance in your mind and allow it to flourish, it is then that it turns into a fortune. Plant that seed right now!

Printed in the United States
By Bookmasters